Reclamation.

A Collection of Poetry by
C. Alexandria-Bernard Thomas

Reclamation.

Copyright © 2022 by C. Alexandria-Bernard Thomas

All Rights Reserved

Printed in the United States of America

Cover by Rich Rocket

Black Minds Publishing is a national publications platform centered around the personal and professional growth of artists and creatives of the Black diaspora. At Black Minds Publishing we aim to give more visibility to raw artistic works, both literary and visual, that center on the healing process of the Black mind, body and spirit. We aren't concerned with the rigid expectations of academia or the "supposed to's" of artistic gatekeepers and instead choose to prioritize genuine works that have meaningful impact for its readers.

Names: C. Alexandria-Bernard Thomas

Title: Reclamation.

Description: Philadelphia, PA: Black Minds Publishing [2022]

Identifiers: 978-1-7375490-5-5

Reclamation.

PUBLISHER'S NOTE

This poetry collection was created from the author's life experiences and imagination.

Without limiting the rights under copyright reserved above, no part of this publication may be reproduced, stored in, or introduced into a retrieval system, or transmitted, in any form, or by any means (electronic, mechanical, photocopying, recording, or otherwise), without the prior written permission of both the copyright owner and the above publisher of this book.

The scanning, uploading, and distribution of this book via the internet or via any other means without permission of the publisher is illegal and punishable by law. Please purchase only authorized electronic editions, and do not participate in or encourage electronic piracy of copyright materials.

Your support of the author's rights is appreciated greatly.

Reclamation.

PRAISE FOR C. ALEXANDRIA-BERNARD THOMAS

C. Alexandria-Bernard Thomas's book Reclamation. is a poetry exposé into the inner workings of "doing the work." This book is unique in the fact that it causes the reader to pause and look at the messy thing that is existing and see the divine; not only in ourselves, but in all the people and things around us. Reclamation. takes us on a journey of growth and release through poetry in the most literal, spiritual, and redemptive way possible. I am glad to have shared in their catharsis.

- Micah the Poet,
Author of *Things No One Else Wants to Say*

Reclamation. is a beautifully written journey of power, strength, and triumphs. C. Alexandria-Bernard Thomas gives you the definition in a vividly painted masterpiece breathing life into the word with a voice that boldly declares; I am here!

- Pi-Anir the Poet,
Author of *To the Goddess in My Garden*

C. Alexandria-Bernard Thomas has words dripping off a powerful pen. I think C. must have added elasticity to the paper used to write this book. Ink this heavy would disintegrate regular paper. This poetry immerses you. Truth and real life are served abundantly. There is no pretense, only raw emotions served with a poetic machete. This is lyrical justice. Words dance with imagery, and occasionally pain cuts in to take the lead then love has the last word.

- Kim B. Miller,
First Black Poet Laureate of Prince William County

Foreword

"Who is C. Alexandria-Bernard Thomas?"

I remember silently asking myself this question in 2020, at the height of the COVID pandemic. I was home, in my bedroom, watching an open mic on Instagram when I first noticed their blonde hair. Immediately, I was intrigued because beyond casually serving a whole look to the interwebs, there was something…different about how they were approaching the moment. As soon as they opened their mouth to speak, I recognized their spirit as familiar. Home, even. And the wildest part was that I didn't even know their full name.

It's hard to imagine that I've only known C. for two years because most days, it feels like lifetimes have danced between us. I can still hear the echo of their laughter from the first time we met, and that sound follows me like lingering perfume in the air, no matter how far from DC I may be at any given moment. Yet, as much as I appreciate their incredible sense of humor, I am most grateful to witness their love and care for the world. Watching C. assume the role of caregiver, nurturer, house muva, advocate, and protector has offered me a window into their soul – and my own. It's rare to meet people who are simply genuine. It's even more rare to meet people who are genuine in living out what they preach. It's almost impossible to meet people who are both. C. is both and beyond.

The architect of Writing to Wellness™, C. has been a fearless leader for myself and so many of my peers in exploring the pains we've endured as new entry points into our creative minds and desires. C. and I have a little game where they will give me an "impossible" writing prompt and I have to complete it within a specified timeframe. I've never been more challenged and mentally stimulated by any arts educator in my life, but I am also, without question or doubt, so much further in my growth because of them and their intention in pushing me to seek the best for myself.
I've had the privilege of watching C. as they journeyed through writing Reclamation. It is born of tears, triumph, frustration, confidence, joy, and love. It is the true embodiment of everything they are and everything I

Reclamation.

know they'll be. When they asked me to write this foreword, my heart almost burst with excitement to not only leave a piece of my love and admiration for one of my favorite writers, but also to have a sneak peek of the entire manuscript ahead of its release. What I've received has been far more than what I can adequately describe in words.

"I memorized me and forgot you". Reclamation. (A six-word story remix). The title poem of this collection rings true to what C. offers to themselves and every person who has the good fortune to encounter Reclamation. C. takes us on a journey through their spirit, traversing hard terrain with the same grace and wit as they take us through the soft and tender moments they hold dearly. Most of all, this collection is packed with space. Space to cry. Space to rejoice. Space to heal. Space to reflect. Space for gratitude. Space for permission. Space to be. To simply be.

I am not who I was prior to reading Reclamation. and I couldn't be more grateful for that truth. As I continue in this life, I will carry the space C. carved out for their readers in this book, and work to not only let go of who and what no longer serves me, but also strive to memorize myself as I am for who I am.

With love,
Najya W.
Author, Performer, and Educator

Reclamation.

Reclamation.

For my brother David, my rock Kendall, my dear Mary Bowman, my House of Bernard children, my forever sisters Saundry and Karmel, my babies Shante and Jessica, all survivors, my joy hearts Micah and Barbz, and my superheroes Safe Shores-The DC Children's Advocacy Center, and Darkness to Light.

Reclamation.

Table of Contents

Glory	17
She	20
This is how prey is trained	24
Cheers	25
Sinew: a pantoum	27
An Ember in the Sky (A poem for Tezzy)	28
13 Lessons	30
i love you.	32
Antihistamine	33
THUG (The Homophobia U Give)	36
Boy	38
Black Queer	40
Reclamation. (A six-word story remix)	41
This Smile	42
Trinity	46
They/Them	48
Mantra	49
Zephyr: a pantoum	51
Who you are!	52
Watch Me Eat	54

Reclamation.

"*The blindfold's off my eyes and now all I see for me is better days.*"

-Janet Jackson, *All for You* album

Reclamation.
Glory
After Lucille Clifton

Come celebrate with me
that every day I survived
every weapon formed
against me.

Reclamation.

Reclamation.

"My mother was the first poem I memorized."

-C. Alexandria-Bernard Thomas

Reclamation.

She

My mother was a strong woman.
Worked her fingers to the bone
day and night. She worked for her children
and barely knew the meaning of the word "rest."
Never minding the fact that she was
sick
weak
and tired of struggling,
she pressed on because she had mouths to feed
and a household to care for.
A household that took her for granted, she skipped not one beat
but that look in her eye
was a screaming plea for help.
Her strength to press and carry on moved my soul
and her smile was a high five from God.
Daily I watched her pull herself from the bed to nurture the world, I mean
her responsibilities.
Her inner pain and failing health was overshadowed by the legacies she
raised.
She knew time would not stand still if she gave up.

Once a month was a hospital stay.
I wonder if she thought of it as a vacation.
But what did I know?
I was a little nappy headed baby who thought their mother was God. when
I was sad she delivered me from it;
her love was church and I glorified in the temple.
Her pill bottles told another story, one I was never able to comprehend.
Two for her heart, one for hypertension and breathing through a tube for
asthma,
each one played her synthetic Jesus and as soon as she got attached, they
fled the scene but my mother was a strong woman.
She knew she was the sarcophagus of the women that flowed through her
veins; their fights; their struggles casted spells for her to go on.

Reclamation.

Her presence—my favorite color,
her laugh— my favorite song,
she was the greatest poem God ever wrote.
No need for edits, he knew she was a rough draft that would author five of the greatest autobiographies ever written. Each one tailored with punctuation marks meant for their life.
She authored each one with the reverse side of every mistake she ever made. Making sure each one was a best seller because my mother was a strong woman.

February 1, 1991, a day I wish I could erase from memory. I woke up to what I thought was Christmas, but December was 10-months away.

I remembered the flashing red lights were part of the chariot that took my mother on vacation.... but this time it felt different.

The feeling I usually felt was replaced with a heavy thump in my stomach awakening my senses to a tremble. My grandfather would not allow me to see my angel before she took leave.

How dare he?

"Go back to your room" was all I heard as the bellhops took her to sanctuary.

Her chariot departed the driveway and I was confused and concerned before I even knew the meaning of the two words.
"Mama," I muttered.

Fast to sleep in my granddaddy's bed,
I had no desire to dream because of this emotional shift.
At the stroke of midnight, a phone call from my sister to my grandfather said mama is gone.

Awakened to hear the news that my main source of compassion would

Reclamation.

never breathe again, I fell back to sleep, a nightmare I refused to claim.

Only ten years old and hearing my mother gone was the first time I ever felt misplaced. So many questions raced through my head and all I could ask was: Why her? I did nothing to deserve this.

Our father, which art in heaven, hallowed be thy name. Thy kingdom come. Thy will be done on earth as it is in heaven.

The prayer she and I shared before she laid me down to sleep,

I pray the lord my soul to keep.

I then heard a verse from her favorite gospel hymn play in my mind, He said come to the water and stand by my side and drink from the fountain you won't be denied and I have seen every teardrop that fell from your eye and I rose to tell you for your tears I died!

So I let my eyes become waterfalls and my memories became clouds I would rest my head upon because she would always be with me.

Although I've seen days that chased away the sun, I knew mama was an angel called home for a greater purpose.
Her vacation turned into a permanent stay and she would finally know the meaning of the word "rest."

And yes, her eternal slumber was well deserved because she would never have to struggle again.

I'm now a sarcophagus of my mother. Her fights; her struggles; casted spells for me to go on.

Her youngest autobiography writing rough drafts with no edits.

No there was no white picket fence with her tending the garden while siblings played cops and robbers in the front yard.

Reclamation.

I'm a proud product of tattered floors, mice and roaches, things that taught me the struggles of life are real and to appreciate all I got.

My mother was a strong woman.

Reclamation.

This is how prey is trained

Bend him until he flimsy nothing.
He means more when he's weak.
His innocence too much child—his
smile has no place here.
Make him loose, easy, unseen—imagined.

Silence his shine, his light too loud.
Crack open, reveal constellations turned
supernova—galaxy be damned.
His sun too bright, too beautiful to be heard.
Take away his sunrise—teach him sunsets
are beneath the horizon.

Bleed him into submission.
Let the beast claim his soul. Transform
his remains, he more than meets the eye.
Carved out archangel, his wings
are for clipping— cursed be his flights.
A pity he will be hole and not whole.

No prayer would want him, no altar
would call for forgiveness— he is sacrifice.
Who is he to deny flesh and blood?
This cocky cum rag— be it life or death,
he is for the taking.

For him, don't be gentle.
Don't be soft.
Show him callous.
Remove remorse.
He is meat—best served tender.

Reclamation.

Cheers

A toast to the man who made me possible
My dad.

You weren't the Antichrist; you were Anti-Chris.

Making me your personal Armageddon.
Leaving me to battle the four horsemen.
Within your paradise I'd never roam, never would my feet touch the soil bearing your fruit—I was forbidden, the one you joyfully, self-righteously cast from your tree.

Thrown away because I wasn't ripe enough for the picking but you cherry-picked fruitful memories that would bar me from the family name and your life.

Learned you took in others to shield your guilt while ignoring the innocent— another counterclockwise turn to the knife in my heart.

I suppose looking at one of your originals was too much for you to bear so you settled for xeroxed images because maybe it looked like a real relationship.

What did I do to make you turn your back so quick?

The only thing you proved to be was the best card shark ever known. In your house of cards, the king had many diamonds, breaking every queen's heart. Keeping an ace up your sleeve, trying not to reveal you were a joker. A crook, a con artist running scams. Embezzling love as conquest trophies— you walked away with gold metals and no remorse.

Father: a man who exercises paternal care over other persons; a paternal protector or provider. That's how Webster defines you. You were nothing more than decades of empty hellos providing broken heartbeats. A destroyer of my heaven and a creator of my hell. I've asked my demons to teach me

Reclamation.

how not to cry over you; it's something this angel needed to know.

So, I raise my glass in honor of never becoming the father you were. May my future children delight in the joy of knowing what it is to be loved unconditionally. May they never feel one is more of a favorite. And may they never question their existence in hopes of getting unwarranted attention to fill voids.

Here's to the man that walked away and never thought once.

Cheers to you dad.

Reclamation.

Sinew: a pantoum

After all, I expected this much
Restless bones no longer still in motionless flesh
Blood thickens, bubbling in this cauldron, desires life
Dig deep in marrow, the answer is within

Restless bones no longer still in motionless flesh
Stretched joints move beyond sound and reach
Dig deep in marrow, the answer is within
Bones crack at sight of becoming new

Stretched joints move beyond sound and reach
Listen to the fibers of tissue bend into shape
Bones crack at sight of becoming new
Vocal is the heart that beats to its calling

Listen to the fibers of tissue bend into shape
Muscles defy gravity, puts smile on face
Vocal is the heart that beats to its calling
After all, I expected this much.

Reclamation.

An Ember in the Sky (A poem for Tezzy)

Let them know you are a sun, God-born.
Center of the universe, put in place by the
hands of the majestic
Blaze across the morning sky.

You are the one.

Life everlasting, tracing clouds bright.
Be it sunrise or sunset,
Silver linings bow to their maker.

You exist to scorch the hearts of those
who have tried to forget you.
They know you, have called you names.
Tried turning you into dusk.

They forget beauty comes in the morning.
Light claims everything it touches– rise always.
Show them you bend shadows into shapes.

You are fearless!

As powerful as the rays of mother,
tough as the core of your father.
Burn with the reminder that you are as bold as
any inferno formed against you. Fire fights fire—ignites with triumph– the dawning of a new smile.

You, the glowing gospel leading flocks to the promised land.

Little wonder.
Anointed treasure.
Kindling kindred.
Joy-made melanin.

Reclamation.

Be great.

Let them know you are a sun, God-born.
Radiant and destined-to-be.
Luminous child darkness will not hold
you.

Reclamation.

13 Lessons

13 Lessons the loves of my life taught me while learning to love myself.

1. Be inspired by the flame but set your own fire. No one likes a repeat.

2. Being popular causes claustrophobia. Don't be a stand in; you were meant to stand out.

3. A walking time bomb of facts. Keeping my brain working with questions, and on a quest for knowledge.

4. But sometimes I wish you would shut the fuck up!

5. You said to stand for something, and to never back down. This is how you earn respect.

6. But think fast and respond slow. Sometimes walking away from a fight is best.

7. You told me I would heal someone with my story. I never knew I'd be the first.

8. You tell me you see beauty every time you're near me. I never knew love would accept me as I am.

9. With you I see rainbows and unicorns. Although they scare me senseless, I'd walk through a field of butterflies to hold you.

10. You made it clear giving up wasn't an option. You believed in me before I believed in myself.

11. You are church when I need a good word. Deliverance from a shattered heart. You called me back to love.

12. You said, "The harder you run from yourself will be the harder you run

Reclamation.

into yourself." I've made it out alive because of you.

13. You are God in human form.

Reclamation.

i love you.

I [sabotage relationships]
Love [makes me think]
You ['re going to abandon me]

Reclamation.

Antihistamine

I was not supposed to fall in love.
Just the thought makes me itch.
It's like I have an allergic reaction to it.
There are no pills or anti-itching creams to help fight this.
So, I won't risk a rash—I avoid it.

A bee sting to my feelings.
Emotions go into anaphylactic shock.
I get choked up the moment I'm shown affection.
My skin flushes at contact.
Lump in my throat from smiling too much.
A nauseating punch to the gut.
I break out in hives.
Can't bear the pain–I'm warm to the touch.

I stand firm in wanting no parts of anyone's heart.
Romantic flutters cause asthma attacks.
Breathe in, breathe out— shallow breaths—I
damn near pass out.

They say big boys don't cry—
I prove them wrong daily.
Put your heart in my hands all
you want…watch me break it.
I'm clumsy…. on purpose.

Purposely falling back if I felt a
twinge of it coming my way.
I hate the responsibility of letting down my guard, trusting someone with
my all and them doing the same.
I've seen relationships fall apart just like that
over spilled milk.
And dammit, I'm lactose intolerant!
Jaded hearts, swollen emotions.

C. Alexandria-Bernard Thomas

Reclamation.

Ain't no love in this house.
I take necessary precautions to protect myself.

But then, here comes you.
You who are not supposed to be here.
You who snuck up on me from out of
nowhere, looking at me like we're destined to be.

An antihistamine for this heartbreaking ragweed.
Showing me roses growing thorns like it's ok!
Have me become hummingbird to honeysuckle.

Tulips in full bloom type of joy.
Nose wide open taking in the sound
of green grass laying beneath us.

Not sure if that tickle is from ladybugs
dancing on my skin or my lonely nights
confessing to be over.

Never imagined a feeling so calm.
This wilderness—at a standstill when
wrapped in your arms. We become
evergreen, long lasting blooming despite
the state of the world.

I run fields just to breathe you in and
Planted firm in our secret garden
palm to palm, heartbeat to heartbeat,
cheek to cheek. I can't get enough of you.

And I like it.

Damn, I love you.

Reclamation.

"You're dedicated to your truth and that is why they fear you."

-C. Alexandria-Bernard Thomas

Reclamation.

THUG (The Homophobia U Give)

You're not born gay; it's a choice.
Be a man!
Can't you walk like a boy!
Put some bass in your voice when you talk!
You so damn so soft!

This ya mamma's fault; she sheltered you.
You know your daddy?
You ain't go no daddy.
If ya did, he wouldn't let you act like this.

You the girl gay?
You wanna to be a girl?
Is that why ya hands on your hips?
Acting like a little sissy.

Keep bending over, you're gonna get AIDS.
Ya know, "Gay Cancer."

You were born a faggot?

Guess you got that gay pride?
What ya proud for?
Always pushing that gay shit in someone's face.
You don't see straight people coming out.
We ain't forcing nothin' on you.
Ain't no straight pride!
I said what ya so proud for!

Wanna hear a joke?
Why shouldn't gay people go to Orlando?
So, they can keep their Pulse. Get it?

You believe in God?

Reclamation.

Go to church?
Pray?

Read the Bible?
Ya know what it says about homosexuality?
I'ma pray for you.

Is this a phase or a cry for attention?
You a child of God but ya going to Hell.
It says so in the Bible!
But I'ma pray for you.

It's Adam and Eve, not Adam and Steve!
Marriage is between man and woman!
Not two men!
Not two women!
Should be a good American Christian marriage!
Why are you against God?

You sure this isn't a phase?
A cry for attention?

I'ma pray for you.

Reclamation.

Boy

Boy, I can tell you're unsettled by my presence. In its bold, colorful, brilliant splendor. This flaming Phoenix, who rises from ashes, catwalks for the gawds, 10's across the board. The audacity to show I'm rainbow after the storm.

You think I don't hear what you say behind my back with your boys. After bragging about the girl you smashed last night but really it was you, Pornhub, and a sock. Defining your masculinity by saying, "He got an ass like a bitch, no homo!" Wearing your saggy jeans and Crayola-colored Reeboks. Makes me beg the question: Who's really tasting the rainbow?

I know you can't handle my confidence to exist. The affirmed smile I wear on the gloomiest of days. The way my voice sings, "Hey girl!" with the sassiest hand wave choreographed by no fucks given. The conviction behind these brown eyes. I know living my truth unsettles you.

And I get it, you're obsessed. With things you can't have. Children always want the most expensive toys, but mama says you can't always get what you want.

So, you throw tantrum, let faggot skydive from your tongue. Test the waters to see how far you can go out and swim. Was told when playing with fire, you get burned and remember I'm a flame and I can set ablaze.

Boy, I have just enough rainbow, with the right size timberland and a torn wife beater for a beat down you won't forget. I swear fo' God you will catch these hands if you try me. Homophobia a bully I bitch slap on the daily. You think you hit bullseye when you play with triggers but playing with triggers can get you shot. So, shut up.

Grow into the man your mama thought you'd be. She carried you in her womb for nine months; you owe her that. Don't be that boy who won't accept "no" from the girl he makes uncomfortable but becomes uncomfortable when he thinks a gay man wants him and then suddenly understands

Reclamation.

consent.

Boy, this isn't my first time at the rodeo. I've been lassoing bulls like you my entire life. Been buck wild with the best of them. Put those cows out to pasture and watched the sunset.

I got a caramel frap, Chipotle and a Netflix and chill situation on deck. Stop disturbing my day with your bullshit. I don't have you to do.

But boy, the next time you see someone as fabulous as me passing you by, I hope your hypermasculinity runs and retreats like those two raisins you call balls. May it learn the importance of being secure with self. And may it learn that catcalling women and them ignoring you don't mean they're playing hard to get.

Cause boy, you deserve that.

Reclamation.

Black Queer

Black Queer born in family of fear.
Cried stardust but painted night with love.
Praised the phases of their shadow for being a guiding light; Black Queer became their own new moon.
The rave unto the most amazing self they know.
Dancing on the axis of a meridian crescent, Black Queer exists.

Reclamation.

Reclamation. (A six-word story remix)

I memorized me and forgot you.

Reclamation.

This Smile
After Mary Bowman

This smile right here ain't no accident.
On purpose is this smile.
Intentional, charismatic, focused,
This smile sexy as fuck.

Bare feet rooted in soil,
Ready for the world is this smile.
Ancestors rejoicing,
Wildest dreams coming true.
This smile is life everlasting.

This smile has a past,
But is present with a future.
This smile exists!

"Be determined," said this smile.
"Ain't nobody got nothing on you," fervent is this smile.
"Yes, Mx. Cunty Hunty," werk this smile.
"All I see for me is better days," shouts this smile.

This smile is affirmation.

I know you love this smile.
Not as much as me.

This smile is confident,
Learned to let go,
Is forgiveness,
Dances like no tomorrow.
Freedom is this smile.

This smile is important,
This smile is kind,

Reclamation.

This smile is smart.

Looks in the mirror and sees my mama
This smile.

I'm here alive with this smile.
I'm a survivor, fall to my knees,
give thanks for this smile.

Never giving up this smile.
Unapologetic is this smile.

Never turned its back,
Looks forward with this smile.
Grateful grateful grateful is this smile.

Cried with this smile,
Became one with this smile,
Stopped pretending to
smile with this smile.

I fought for this smile.

I love this smile.

C. Alexandria-Bernard Thomas

Reclamation.

Reclamation.

"Poetry not only saved my life, but it gave me the power to say my abuse wasn't my fault."

-C. Alexandria-Bernard Thomas

Reclamation.

Trinity

I.

Born on a Thursday, at the crack of night, where an evening sky knew their name before it was law. Bowed before heaven, a mixture of souls played airbender breathing life into what grace allowed to lay upon thee. Held together by prayer, kept secret by sin— a collection of hymns stashed in the creases of a smile bound by scripture. A reflection of their mother's imperfections, the footprints of their father's flaws was a blessing born on a Thursday, at the crack of night, where an evening sky knew their name before it was law.

II.

Have I always settled for less than I deserve? Have I given of myself freely? Have I held sorrow in the form of strangers? Have I ignored red flags waving in danger? Have I sacrificed my existence and become void? Have I forgotten me to memorize you? Have I realized you never loved me? Have I known this but been too afraid? Have I forgiven myself completely? Have I owned my insecurities? Have I become the person I knew I'd be? Have I always known this but been too afraid? Well?

III.

I am fire laughing at water.
I am sound climbing off the walls of teeth.
I am a star guiding the waves of oceans.
I am joy filled with the faith of a mustard seed.
I am testimony on tried-and-true days.
I am gospel hummed over Sunday dinner.
I am a lotus pushing through the thickest of mud.
I am shelter from the coldest of winters.
I am ending generational trauma.
I am my past and my present, birthing my destiny.
I am the harmony from your favorite song.

Reclamation.

I am not afraid of your weapons formed against me.
I am alive on purpose.
I am purpose, ferociously.
I am all I never could imagine.
I am magnificently me.

Reclamation.

They/Them

I.

They shook the earth still upon first breath. Held steady the winds with a roar chasing fireflies into midnight. With the flash of a smile pulled winter from oceans, the shine in their eyes whispered fire into existence. A precious child born of wonders; miracles dripped from their fingertips.

Not knowing they would be robbed of their nectar by many.

II.

You taught them to bury their questions. To turn answers into stone if they stared directly at truth. Told them their enemies deserved silence, not the rattle of a tongue pleading for peace. Made war out of their laughter. Keeping aim to strike blows. Showing them wrecking balls are stronger than any boundary they put into place. Made them hand over their consent, while tucking them in between your teeth.

How else could you soften them for the world to eat?

Reclamation.

Mantra

They listen.
They hear.
They cry.
They rejoice.
They breathe.

They begin to

Live.
Love.
Smile.
Laugh.
Forgive.

They found joy

In sunshine.
Became full moon incarnate.
Rainwater tap dancing.
A thunderous applause.

They are powerful.

In growing.
And willing.
And trusting.

They are human

Being patient.
Calm with peace
They are whole.
They are nurturer.
They are giver.

Reclamation.

They are provider.
They are child.
They are sibling.
They are pibling.
They are muva.
They are great.

They are open arms.

Reclamation.

Zephyr: a pantoum

With arms open, eyes closed wide, inhale and leap
Fervent are the hands reaching to Heaven
Steadfast is the soul against the back of zephyr
Give into this salvation where air meets sound

Fervent are the hands reaching to Heaven
Eye to eye with dawn, angels orchestrate light
Give into this salvation where air meets sound
Architect of the wind becomes guardian of flight

Eye to eye with dawn, angels orchestrate light
Hold tight to the breeze, it knew you before the womb
Architect of the wind becomes guardian of flight
Majestic are the wings sculpting air into shape

Hold tight to the breeze, it knew you before the womb
Carrying you where mountain tops await your arrival
Majestic are the wings sculpting air into shape
Relax your legs, this moment you won't need them

Today, you're a miracle, mountain tops await your arrival
All you need to do is fly, even if it seems impossible
Relax your legs, this moment you won't need them
The first step, easy, defeating comforts pull

Fly, even if it seems impossible, you got this
Next, learn to trust the breeze beneath your wings
The first step, easy, defeating comforts pull
Keep your arms open, eyes closed wide, inhale and leap.

Reclamation.

Who you are!

My reflection told me I'd given up on what's important.
Was concerned of no sign of belief in self.
Said I dreamt in sorrow, no longer in hope.
Colored with hate, chasing away the true blue of my beating heart.
My reflection told me I accepted being lackluster over the greatness sworn to me.

No sound in those beautiful brown eyes,
they used to sing songs over Captain Crunch
and Saturday morning cartoons.
A faded smile when greeting the sun.
No shine, just a dim clicking of teeth.
A low glow radiant tone when speaking.

Why have I settled?
Forgotten who I am?
Accepted tragedy over triumph?
Chris, you are a gift from God!
From conception, greatness was spoken over you.

There are prayers tucked under your eyelids.
When you cry, your blessings, they shower you.
You were built from the backs of elders.
They fought so you could stand.
Sacrificial war cries made to protect you.
If "I wish you would" was a person, it would be you.

Told me my name still bends with confidence. Fortresses are the syllables housing its presence. There's a flame burning behind this voice, scorching the evil formed against me.
My reflection said, "There will be no tragedy
when the divine has promised life to someone they created."
Do you know who you are?
From where you have come?

Reclamation.

The pits of hell that tried to claim you failed.
Your glow, baptized fire.
Don't give in when you weren't put out.
Remember who you are!
Black glowing Joy! Happy and free.
Scream your name from mountain tops.

You were forged in the belly of a black diamond,
no stone could shimmer as brave as you.

Your mama is proud.

You are the fight proving rejection should fear your existence.
Your pain may know you, but it has no power over you.

Your brother, David, is proud.

Go, plant your feet, chest out, shoulders back,
head held high. Smile until your shine meets the sun!

Remember who you are!

You are graceful!
You are bold!
You are color!
You are magic!
You are sound!
You are magnificent!
You are hope
You are the ancestors' promise!
You are Margaret's fifth creation.
C. Alexandria-Bernard Thomas!
Remember who you are!
And don't you ever forget it!

Reclamation.
Watch Me Eat

I remember being asked, "What makes
you think you have a seat at this table?"

Was told "You'll never be on stage,
your work mediocre at best."

It was written, "You think you doing something
with your poetry. You ain't no monster with the pen."

DM's that read "You a runt playing dress up.
Sit your ass down somewhere with that bullshit!"

And I heard you. Loud and clear.

Being put in time out by broken
clocks that never ticked ain't my thing.

Since 13, I've bent emotions into words
Made fortress out of storm clouds.
Made pain learn my name before it taught
me how to walk.

Put my soul on stage, bled so I can breathe.
Made kaleidoscope out of applause that hang
from my neck.

Ate with Dr. Giovanni, high-fived
Ms. Finney. Swedish royalty greeted
me with my name tattooed on their tongues.

Serve face for those who sneer at me.
The same ones who act like they know.
Who better to tell my story than me?
Who better to know my worth?

Reclamation.

Who better to give shape to their sky?

Your splinter made table could never seat me,
let alone hold my plate.

Wake up black, queer, non-binary daily.
Had to fight!
And did!
And won!

What's a guppy to a savage?

Never wanted to be a monster.
Rather a slayer to the very thing
haunting my peace.
Enticing my fear.
DMing my trauma.

Face to face with the ogres who try me constantly.
Who made choice to ignore warning signs
that read, "Don't come for me."

What's a match to a volcano?

I erupt to show others it's ok
to be golden and blue at the same time.

Praise them for sacrificing
their egos on the same stage
you tried to claim.

The one you said you owned.
Give the same little dick energy too,
Week after week, reaching for applause.

A mouse with a crayon at best.

C. Alexandria-Bernard Thomas

Reclamation.

All you are is a
reminder for why I glow.
Be everything you can't.
Savior
Human
Real
Liberated
ME

Ain't nothing you could do to me that ain't
already been done.
Ain't nothing you can say that could make me
back off.
Ain't nothing about your vapid existence that
will make me quiver.

MEMO: Fuck your table!

Don't let the sage and crystals fool you.
You don't need this rumble!
Stay in your lane before you cause an accident.

And that's on my humility.

Reclamation.

www.ingramcontent.com/pod-product-compliance
Lightning Source LLC
Chambersburg PA
CBHW070942160426
43193CB00011B/1780